Love Matters

Ocean Shackleton

Love Matters Ministries
Lyons, Ohio

Published by Love Matters Ministries
505 North Adrian Street
Lyons, Ohio 43533

Love Matters
ISBN 978-0692200292

This book is dedicated to Virginia Lee Lintner,
Mother Extraordinaire.

Acknowledgements

All my life, I have written poetry and, over time, I accumulated thousands of poems. For many years, friends have urged me to write a book.

Now, thanks to the insistence and persistence of my good friends, Pat and Larry Downing, and thanks to Pat's able assistance, here, for the first time, is a collection of my poetry.

Foreword

The poetry in this collection represents bits and pieces of a life-long accumulation. Beginning at an early age, Ocean observed his world and his own responses, and he preserved his impressions in poetry.

He has participated in many groups around the country, often winning the title of "Poet of the Month" with Poetry in the Woods in Ft. Lauderdale, Florida, and twice "Poet of the Year" with the East Coast Academy of Poets.

Ocean calls much of his poetry "snapshots," as they depict particular people or moments in eternity. He has been published in numerous anthologies, magazines and newspapers around the country.

This book is the first compilation of his poetry.

Patricia Downing
Asheville, North Carolina

Contents

BROKEN:

Looking

Tuning In

Exhaustion grips the pen and hand
and embraces the brain in an iron band.
Though I seek to write something deep,
I find myself falling fast asleep thinking of
whether or not you're real
or simply an emotion that I feel.

It's like you are found on another plane,
like a radio tuner's changing channels again.
Just because I can't see you doesn't mean you're not there.
When I tune in one channel
you're still "on the air."

But my tuner's not working,
or at least, so it seems,
because I can only find you
in the land of my dreams.

Are you a dream or reality?
Whichever – you are, you are gone from me,
and I keep changing channels
trying to find you.

Laughter

Laughter, the ambrosia of life,
bubbling effervescently as she spins
the corkscrew into the colorful long-necked
bottle of wine in preparation for her
coming-out party at Zuma.

Slowly the crowd begins to gather.
The floor is bared for dancing,
perhaps for some romancing.
It all appears entrancing
as faux nymphs and satyrs gather
across the street from where
Bacchus holds sway on a
glorious Friday night.

Cloud appreciation is evident
but none are present here
save impressions in oil.

Josie shines as bright as any moon.

Ode to the Artist

Cowboy boots and distant clouds
while, nearby, a hawk is soaring.
You may say of her many things
but never say "She's boring."

As filled with life and vibrancy
as a thundering cataract.
Mystical as the dragonfly
and pleasing to a feller's eye,
but all over the track.

She races to the bunkhouse,
leaps upon her horse and rides
in all directions simultaneously.

Hooray for her energy.
Like a Texas tornado racing across
Hill Country.

She Smiles

She smiles and it's like a new moon rising,
full of promise of brightness.

Her eyes shimmer in quiet conversation
which approaches a thunderous roar.
The thunder of that silence is like an earthquake
8.6 on the Richter scale that vibrates the
entire universe to its very core.

She reminds me of every party I never
attended. I am a constant captive of those
infinitely captivating eyes.

Memories of a "P. K."
(Preacher's Kid)

The minister's daughter
was very hot.
I thought her virtuous.
She was not.

She drove me home
from the church one night.
My mother awakened
to quite a sight.

Two nude bodies
quite entangled,
her foot in the steering wheel,
nearly mangled,
attempting desperately
to get it free
while the horn was blasting
mightily.

Be sure the truth shall find you out.
The world will discover what you're about.

Artist's View

The charcoal and the canvas
are waiting to capture
my impressions of you,
the feelings of rapture.

Skin – the texture of music
on a warm summer's night.
Eyes like dewdrops on roses
in the morning's bright light.

The most difficult task
and the hardest to capture
is the glow from within you
that causes the rapture.

Your lips - the texture of petals of flowers,
I dream of them brushing my own lips for hours.

My vision like an acid trip carries me away.
I lust for the canvas and what it may say.

Cameo

Like a classic cameo, she seems
carved deep in the stuff of dreams.
Classic form and classic beauty
of a form one should find suiting
for the carving of a cameo.

Reflections of Athena or Diana:
They're the faces I recall.
She is more than representative
of these Greek classics, all.

How the artist would yearn for more ivory or bone
to capture the visage before it is gone.

She smiles and the Mona Lisa pales beside her.
Her eyes flash brilliant in the tavern's light.

Her chestnut hair spills like a waterfall,
splashing off her shoulders spilling across her breast.

Falling tresses, a flowing stream,
reflect the padded moon's soft beam.
Her smile complements its frown
as her chestnut wealth comes spilling down.

What a treasure she possesses
in that warm flood of chestnut tresses.

Lost in the Music

I get lost in the music she plays
as she tinkles the ivories and sings,
producing a warmth like the sun's golden rays.
I rejoice in the pleasure it brings.

Notes spill forth like a tinkling stream
in its burbling trips down the mountain,
like fairy laughter creating a dream
of a moonbeamed rainbowed fountain.

Wrapped in reverie as those notes start to fade,
I trip on the laughter that spills ever after
and swim in the music she's made.

Detroit

In the city park, lying in the noonday sun,
your blouse pulled from your skirt.
The sun beats hot upon a bare midriff
which has seen the sun before.

I remember other times,
fewer layers of tan.

Licking lips in anticipation, I remember the saltiness
as my lips grazed sun warmed skin,
while tiny beads of perspiration
formed upon it.

What Lies Beneath

A tattoo peeps from the edge of her dress
creating the question of what remains hidden.
And in flights of fancy, each of us guess
at the balance of art work as though we are bidden.

It's like the famous game show host
who calls out "Come on down."
We guess is it the least or most
or how much more may be found
there beneath that undulating sheath.
We're called to ask, "What lies beneath?"

Silently slipping through the room
in a seductive sheath,
movements so intriguing.
Ah! What lies beneath?

We may each envision it, as everyone knows.
She is buck naked
beneath her clothes.

Communication

The sound of the drum and all the singing
prevented conversation. Our ears were ringing.

She asked me a question I could not ascertain.
I wanted to communicate
and willing to take pain,
but with all the racket going on
I couldn't get her name.

I was told she was from Hendersonville,
but with all the noise, I missed her.
Verbal communication was impossible,
so I kissed her.

I don't know what possessed me
as I'd not done that before.
The lady had impressed me
and perhaps I should implore
forgiveness, but I'm really not ashamed,
though I believe it would be wiser
if, at first, I learned her name.

Mountain Woman

It's two AM and very dark,
but I can't close my eyes.
I toss and turn. For you I yearn,
a desire I can't disguise.

Since my eyes first beheld you,
you've occupied my mind.
I've seen you in the fluffy clouds
and in ten thousand lights.
My days have all been filled with you,
and so my restless nights.

The world's become a mirror,
I see you everywhere.
Your smile reflects from every glass,
your skin, your eyes, your hair.

I feel your pulse, it throbs with mine.
In each beat of my heart
a fire burns that would consume
all that keeps us apart.

It's three AM and I lie here
hearing your voice singing,
and the strains of "Mountain Birth"
may never stop their ringing.

They ring within the "Secret Garden"
deep within my soul,
reverberating like the tuning fork
that rings a crystal bowl.

The note you are a matching tone
that stirs my every cell.
I vibrate the same frequency,
like the ringing of a bell
that tolls between two mountains,
each echoing the tone
until they merge in subtle waves
and harmonize as one.

It's four AM and in the rain
that splatters against my window pain,
I hear guitar notes and look outside
in time to see your figure glide
across a meadow filled with flowers
as you play and sing and dance.

The mountains in the background
serve only to enhance.
You're like the mountain butterfly
that dances in the air,
and everywhere that I may look
I see you whirling there.

Mountain woman you have won me.
Your laugh, your smile, your grace
thrill me, fill me constantly.
I see your smiling face.

Exhaustion overwhelms me
and at last I fall asleep
dreaming dreams of you, my mountain woman,
instead of counting sheep.

Magnetism

Your neck draws me like a magnet,
so soft and warm and white.
It appears to be so sensual,
I lie awake at night
thinking of you and how it would be
to be your lover:
Touching you, caressing you, creating a joyous experience
full of passion, sensuality and wonder.

Shackleton, Ocean, charcoal sketch, 2014, detail from a larger work, Rembrandt van Rijn, *Bathsheba at Her Bath*, 1654, oil on canvas.

Loving

Waiting

Give me back the life I spent waiting.
Wasting life, precious moment by moment.
Waiting until I thought I had all I needed
to experience life,
while the experience of life I had was
waiting.

Waiting, waiting, waiting, why?
The thunder of a big bass drum... the rush of the
wind ... and the tinkle of raindrops.
The summer storm is on us.

How much life has passed us by, waiting for
the rains that never came?
How many picnics have we missed because
it might rain?

Remember when we did go, and it did rain,
and the two of us were caught, soaking wet
as we ran to the summer house?

Remember how the steam rose from us both,
locked in each other's arms?

The Dance of Intimacy

We dance the dance of intimacy
and in its sweet embrace,
we touch each other's souls and see
we're, each one, in our place.

Loving is the great command
but when lost and alone,
we don't know how to take our stand
and we have to be shown.

So show us, Divine Wisdom,
in the way we'll hear it.
With rapt intent we listen
to receive the voice of Spirit.

Heart Space

The sound of love is in a sigh
while tears are forming in the eye,
the colors of violet and blue
within the heart ring warm and true,
the sound of waves that break in sighing
while the softness nests in crying.

The Magic Mustache Ride

Very slowly I awaken
from a long night of lovemaking
and find you pressed against my skin.
I feel your energy come in.

Your fingers brush my pubic hair.
I feel ecstatic shock waves there
and relive with much sensation
the throws of last night's love creation.

Looking up through pubic hair to see
your love-glazed eyes looking down at me.
While you are on the mustache ride,
I taste what you are like inside.

I read your body like a map
from here to lands of ecstasy,
and then we take a little nap
'til you, once more, have need of me.

I move my fingers through your hair.
The sensual button hidden there
responds and you begin to writhe and twist.
You lose all will then to resist,
and caught within this moving tide
you mount the magic mustache ride.

With rhythmic motion
like a fast grandfather's clock,

my tongue contacts your clitoris,
tick tock tick tock tick tock.

The fingers of your hungry hands
trace my skin like burning brands.
In the erotic paths they take,
each one leaves a burning wake.

Your hands clutch at me frantically
like waves, the shore, from stormy sea.
Then a shudder like a tidal wave
wells up as from some sub-sea cave.

You quake like trees in hurricane,
gasping cries of joy or pain.
Hungrily, you climb upon my hips.
Breasts rise and fall like storm tossed ships.

Then just as if the storm had passed,
you collapse in gentle waves at last,
'til again that voice from deep inside
calls you to the mustache ride.

Oft have I prayed at Heaven's gate
for results which, sometimes early, sometimes late,
were most important, oft earthshaking
but at the least, were worth the making.

She who would make her prayers with me
oft responded mightily
and wherever possible, nightly.

How often I've found myself there,
given over to that fervent prayer,
the object of my great devotion
lost in her erotic motion.

"A loaf of bread, a jug of wine and Thou."

from *The Rubaiyat of Omar Khayyam*
translated by Edward FitzGerald

Skinny Dipping

With our wrapping all undone,
we lie naked in the sun
on top of Earth's green sod.
There we feel the kiss of God.

Your hands glide along my skin.
I feel your energy come in.
In fact I feel, in whole or part,
feelings deep within your heart.

En masse we lie upon the lawn,
our emotions rolling on
until they reach their loving crest
and we each realize "We're blessed."

We share our laughter and our fears,
are lost within a flood of tears,
then all that we can find thereafter
is the joy and loving laughter.

Tuesdays

What day ever could be better?
It has me chafing at the bit.
Tuesday's mine in any weather.
I get the best outcome from it.

She's so fair, freckled and sweet.
How I yearn for when we meet.
Trained by spirits from above,
she is made for making love.

Time with her sure to uplift,
she views each lover as a gift.
"So many men, so little time,"
that is her one cause sublime.

She chose a man for every day.
Seven men can't stay away.
That special way she kneels in greeting,
I so anticipate every meeting.

She does not require dining.
A hamburg or hotdog leaves her shining,
beaming with the joy of being
this sexy angel I've been seeing.

"Mon Petit," so full of life,
she would not be one man's wife.
She always loved to play the field,
through which so much has been revealed.

The *Kama Sutra* didn't know
the lovemaking tricks that she'd bestow.
Making love so wild and free,
and Tuesdays are reserved for me!

Sans Canvas

She sits there looking like a picture,
a challenge for the artist within.
I'm called to charcoal and the canvas,
so let the work begin.

How to capture such an image
and let the canvas speak,
like wrestling in some football scrimmage
to arrive at what I seek.
The challenge stands as a salute
to extra-ordinary beauty.

Not possessing paint or canvas
and somewhat in a rush,
I use the pen and paper,
sans canvas and sans brush.

Webs

In the soft grey morning light
the webs of sleep left from the night.
Your body fits mine like a glove,
adhered to me with webs of love.

Sweet faint chords of love's connection,
woven throughout life's perfection.
The rightness of our connected being
makes strong the threads that I am seeing.

I lie here wanting to recapture
the waves we make of divine rapture
when in our joining ecstasy,
I feel you become one with me.

Phyllis

There's a halo round her face.
She looks at me and smiles.
Her presence brightens up this place
and it has for a while.

Her hands are clasped as if in prayer.
It's obvious there's power there.
She has forged a strong connection
leading to her resurrection.

I sought for her a long, long time.
I am so grateful she is mine.

Broken

Time

Time is flowing like a river
spilling down a mountain,
a roaring, raging torrent now
that once was just a fountain.

Friends and family swept away
that long withstood the flood,
and the places where they were
are now just flats of mud.

Muddier the memories of many,
while of some there aren't any
traces left of how we were –
no reflections left of him or her.

"Where have all the flowers gone,
long time passing?
Where have all the flowers gone,
Long time ago?"

Quotation is from the song "Where Have All the Flowers
Gone?" by Pete Seeger, 1955

Faded Brilliance

We gazed a while upon the sun,
warm bright orb but blinding.
Brilliant pleasures overdone,
now darkness we are finding.

Knight errant and Lady Guinevere
questing for the Holy Grail.
Do they really ever find it?
Does anyone?

To be Holy, whole, wholly myself.
I wonder. I do not choose to be
a common man, I choose to be
uncommon if I can.

Peer pressure wants all cattle to be brown.
Does one dare to be different?
Eight to five – pay on Friday,
not a high day.
Ocean day with a briny breeze,
wading day up to the knees.

Breakup

Last night I cried when I spoke with you.
There's a tear in the fabric of my soul.
I let you inside me where no one has been.
You found me wanting and threw me out.

I trusted you with parts of me
that I've trusted to no one before.
Now I feel soiled and viley despoiled
and you've thrown me out the door.

You told me you loved me
much bigger than life
and repeated the promise of Ruth,
and spoke of the sea birds
and mating for life.
Then one day you say
you're no longer my wife.

The Stone

You asked me if I was cold,
and I am not,
yet deep inside a cold wind blows
in a vast vacant spot,
a place where few have ever been,
a very privileged few.

On one hand I could count them all,
though one of them was you.
Holy of holies deep inside
the door now closed is locked.
Because of all that has transpired,
the true heart route is blocked.

Months and years I've slaved and sweat
to roll the stone away.
Today it rolled back by itself and
looks like it will stay.
Heavy stone, heavier heart
scarred and withered much apart.

Mayday

Unhomed, evicted from my space
where first I had belonged.
Unwelcome, by myself, unwanted,
gone now the warbled song
that for years I have been singing:
"I belong, I belong here."
Like a slap that still is stinging
accompanied by waves of fear.

Fading purpose, draining meaning
accompanied by an inner keening -
a wail, a shriek, a silent scream.
What can all this turmoil mean?

Lost, alone, confused, afraid,
a whirling cyclone in my brain.
I want to run away from home,
but where is that?
I'm so alone.

The Chasm

Folding back the flowered spread
I lay down on my double bed,
a barren place, a desert waste.
I toss and turn and sleep in haste.

It is an endless broad plateau,
as I lie there it seems to grow.
I fear the vastness of this space
in which I used to see your face.

I'd reach for you and find you there,
and now I grapple empty air.
Sometimes I feel a chasm, black,
where once you lay upon your back,
and if I reach for you I know
I'll fall endlessly to rocks below.
So I cannot sleep at all,
afraid that I may roll and fall.

I seek your presence everywhere,
hungering to stroke your hair,
fingers raking empty air,
multiplied emptiness there.

It's Raining

It's raining out. I weep within.
I don't know how I should begin
to tell the tale I have to tell
and in its telling do it well.

My tears within, a massive tide,
tidal waves of tears I've cried.
An ebb and flow that floods my soul
with wrenching sobs that leave me cold.

Lost, alone, confused, afraid
by the decisions I have made
which carried me to where I stand,
drowning out of sight of land.

I placed my loving hopes in you,
while you, you said you loved me too.
My dreams of happy ever after
awash in tears that drown the laughter.

I knew that we'd be great together,
but here I am in rainy weather.
It's raining out. I weep within,
just don't know how to begin.

Alone After Ten

It's after ten and all alone
I sit and meditate upon
a crystal ball held by a unicorn.

I see the spectrum there
and muse on bands of color
that shoot piercing through the air.

I feel a vastness to the space
the air around me fills.
I miss your laughter and your face.
The night air gives me chills.

Alone, so alone after ten on Sunday
to bed with just a panda bear,
wishing you were there.

My left shoulder has never
felt so empty.

Alone, after ten.
Your line is busy.

Goodbye, My Love

That's it today,
the only words I've left to say.
Know that I wish for you and yours
the best.
I leave it to God to provide
the rest.

I go to find His place
and peace for me
in some healing spot
beside some sea,
where the salt laden breeze
sings a lullaby
with the pulsing waves
and the seagulls' cry,
where the waves and the sun
can provide a start
for the balm that may heal
a broken heart.

Ocean Shackleton

Born June 8, 1938 to Herbert Skirving and Virginia Lee Shackleton in Abington, Pennsylvania, Ocean was the first of four children, followed by Herb, Ginnie, and Mary, his siblings.

Following a tumultuous childhood, he enlisted in the United States Army as a 17-year-old, at the request of his mother, step-father and a judge. He served three years in Germany, developing an affinity for the language, and he was discharged in New Jersey in April, 1959.

Ocean worked in manufacturing and landscaping, and he also made his living as an artist, a tree surgeon, bar tender, waiter, Maitre d,' cook, chef, house painter, journeyman carpenter, general contractor, alcoholism counsellor and treatment-center manager. Throughout his life, he continued to write poetry, committing to paper his observations of life and his thoughts and feelings..

During the 24 years he lived in the mountains of Western North Carolina, Ocean often shared his poems at local gatherings, and in 2017, he earned the silver medal for poetry in the Western North Carolina Senior Games. He now lives in a small village in northwestern Ohio with his sweetheart, Nancy, her father, Charles, and six cats. He continues to write and create art, and is still active in several community organizations.

Want More of Ocean's Poetry?

If you enjoyed this book of poems, you may also appreciate Ocean's second volume, *Gratitude Journey*. For over 44 years, he has been on a journey of inner transformation.

These poems reflect that long inner journey. Written over several years, they contain his insights into his relationship with himself, other people and the higher power at work in his life.

Steps in his journey included grieving, forgiveness, gratitude, love, awareness of the power of words, self-evaluation, and the constant presence of a powerful, loving intelligence at every step.

These poems offer insights that will uplift and inspire you along your journey.

His next volume, in progress, is *Ocean:* poems and stories of the sea.

www.ingramcontent.com/pod-product-compliance
Lightning Source LLC
Chambersburg PA
CBHW071642050426
42443CB00026B/939